Edward Snowden

NSA Contractor and Whistle-Blower

Fiona Young-Brown

Cavendish Square

New York

Published in 2019 by Cavendish Square Publishing, LLC
243 5th Avenue, Suite 136, New York, NY 10016

Library of Congress Cataloging-in-Publication Data

Names: Young-Brown, Fiona author.
Title: Edward Snowden : NSA contractor and whistle-blower / Fiona Young-Brown.
Description: First Edition. | New York : Cavendish Square Publishing, LLC, 2019. |
Series: Hero or villain?: Claims and counterclaims | Includes webography. |
Includes bibliographical references and index. | Audience: Grades: 7-12.
Identifiers: LCCN 2018001389 (print) | LCCN 2018004808 (ebook) |
ISBN 9781502635396 (ebook) | ISBN 9781502635389 (library bound) |
ISBN 9781502635402 (paperback)
Subjects: LCSH: Snowden, Edward J., 1983---Juvenile literature. |
WikiLeaks (Organization)--Biography--Juvenile literature. |
United States. National Security Agency/Central Security Service--Juvenile literature. |
Whistle blowing--United States--Biography--Juvenile literature. |
Leaks (Disclosure of information)--United States--Juvenile literature. |
Electronic surveillance--United States--Juvenile literature. |
Domestic intelligence--United States--Juvenile literature.
Classification: LCC JF1525.W45 (ebook) | LCC JF1525.W45 Y68 2018 (print) |
DDC 327.12730092 [B] --dc23
LC record available at https://lccn.loc.gov/2018001389

Editorial Director: David McNamara
Editor: Michael Spitz
Copy Editor: Rebecca Rohan
Associate Art Director: Amy Greenan
Designer: Amy Greenan/Christina Shults
Production Coordinator: Karol Szymczuk
Photo Research: J8 Media

The photographs in this book are used by permission and through the courtesy of: Cover, p. 34 Kyodo/AP Images; p. 4 Lenscap Photography/Shutterstock.com; p. 5 (and throughout the book) Wikimedia Commons/File:Cantino planisphere (1502).jpg/Public Domain; p. 7 Barton Gellman/Getty Images; p. 8 Philippe Lopez/AFP/Getty Images; p. 10 Carol Highsmith/Library of Congress/Wikimedia Commons/File:Aerial view of CIA headquarters, Langley, Virginia 14760v.jpg/Public Domain; p. 12 Spencer Platt/Getty Images; p. 15 Lukiyanova Natalia Frenta/Shutterstock.com; p. 16 Sgt. Roman/US Army/The LIFE Picture Collection/Getty Images; p. 20-21 Bettmann/Getty Images; p. 29 Chris Kleponis/Bloomberg/Getty Images; p. 39 The Asahi Shimbun/Getty Images; p. 40 Evaristo Sa/AFP/Getty Images; p. 42 Ted Soqui/Corbis/Getty Images; p. 46-47 Anthony Wallace/AFP/Getty Images; p. 52 Epsilon/Getty Images; p. 56 Bryan Bedder/Getty Images for The New Yorker; p. 60 Harry Hamburg/NY Daily News Archive/Getty Images; p. 63 Thos Robinson/Getty Images for The New Yorker; p. 66 MPI/Getty Images; p. 70-71 Sharrett/Getty Images; p. 77 Bruno Vincent/Getty Images; p. 81 Gabe Ginsberg/WireImage/Getty Images; p. 88 Jupiterimages/Creatas/Thinkstock.com; p. 92-93 Richard Levine/Alamy Stock Photo; p. 96 Richard Shotwell/Invision for Open Road/AP Images; p. 98 Kenzo Tribouillard/AFP/Getty Images.

Printed in the United States of America

CON TENTS

Chapter One   5
Introduction to a Whistle-Blower

Chapter Two   13
What Led to Snowden's Actions?

Chapter Three   35
Snowden's Leaks

Chapter Four   57
Edward Snowden: Hero or Villain

Chapter Five   89
Summing Up

Glossary   100
Chronology   102
Further Information   104
Selected Bibliography   106
Index   110
About the Author   112

Several newspapers from the United Kingdom, including the *Guardian*

Introduction to a Whistle-Blower

On June 6, 2013, a headline on the front page of the *Guardian*, a British newspaper, kicked off a controversy that would cause a public uproar and send international intelligence agencies scrambling to protect themselves. It read: "NSA Collecting Phone Records of Millions of Verizon Customers Daily." The story, by journalist Glenn Greenwald, revealed that the National Security Agency (NSA) had obtained a top-secret court order that allowed them to gather the telephone records of US customers. As the news spread, people asked themselves, "Who has my private data, and why?"

Over the next twelve months, more than two hundred related stories appeared in the *Guardian*. Other newspapers followed suit. The *Washington Post*, the *New York Times*, *Der Spiegel*, and *Le Monde* are just a few of the leading global publications that shared stories and information questioning the overreaching security protocols in place since the September 11, 2001, attacks on the World Trade Center and the Pentagon in the United States. When did national security override personal privacy? Why would nations spy on their own citizens?

Equally tantalizing was the story of the man behind the revelations. Who was he, and what were his motives? With regards to his identity, he had made no attempts to remain anonymous. Soon, the entire world would know the name of Edward Snowden.

Early Life

Edward Joseph Snowden was born in North Carolina on June 21, 1983. He was born into a family whose members dedicated themselves to government service, some in the judiciary and others in the military and the FBI. In the beginning, Snowden showed few signs of distinguishing himself. He failed to graduate high school, instead completing his GED and taking a few additional classes at the local community college. After his parents divorced, he spent much of his time in relative isolation, glued to his computer screen and participating in online chat rooms. He took a few university classes online but never earned a degree. He showed a strong aptitude for computers and expressed a keen interest in Japanese culture.

In 2004, Snowden showed signs of following in his family's footsteps when he enlisted in a special military recruitment program to train for the Special Forces. He did not complete training, claiming to have broken both legs.

In December 2013, Edward Snowden gave his first interview since being granted asylum in Russia.

The *South China Morning Post*'s website published its interview with Edward Snowden, revealing NSA hacking in China, on June 13, 2013.

After a stint as a security guard at the University of Maryland's Center for Advanced Study of Languages, he was able to get a job in the global communications division of the Central Intelligence Agency (CIA) in Langley, Virginia. Whether this was due to his exceptional technical skills or through family influence has been debated. Nevertheless, he received a security clearance and was a US federal employee. He worked for the CIA for the next three years, enjoying the perks of an international posting. In 2009, he resigned and went to work for the computer company Dell at their facility in Tokyo. Dell worked extensively with the NSA, and Snowden says that his role was to help educate military and government facilities so that they might protect themselves from hackers.

Leaking Documents and Repercussions

By 2012, Snowden was working at Dell's NSA regional operations center in Hawaii, with a level of clearance that gave him access to highly sensitive documents. It may have been a surprise to some when he left his job at Dell in 2013 and took a lower-paying job with Booz Allen Hamilton, an information technology consulting firm that was also a subcontractor to the NSA. The biggest surprise came just a few months later.

On May 20, 2013, Snowden called his supervisors at work to say that he was sick. He then caught a plane from Hawaii to Hong Kong. That was the last time he would be on US soil. Once in Hong Kong, he met with three political

The Central Intelligence Agency (CIA) is headquartered in Langley, Virginia.

journalists and began the process of leaking thousands of classified NSA documents, beginning with those that led to the shocking headline in the *Guardian*.

The exact number of documents that Snowden stole may never be known. Some estimates say several thousand, while others speculate that he could have retrieved up to half a million files. Should he return to the United States, Snowden faces several charges from the government, including violating the Espionage Act of 1917 and theft of government property. At the time of this writing, he remains in Moscow, Russia, where he has been granted asylum since the summer of 2013. His asylum request has been extended until 2020, and details of his life in Russia are few and far between.

It's important to look at what global events precipitated Snowden's actions—in particular, the September 11 attacks and how they changed laws regarding surveillance in the United States. It's also important to look at what changes his revelations might have brought about. Is Edward Snowden a patriotic hero or a traitor, or is the truth somewhere in between?

National Security Agency

The National Security Agency (NSA) was officially formed in 1952 by President Harry Truman, but its origins go back to the First World War, when an organization was first tasked with deciphering coded messages sent by the enemy. Upon its creation, the agency was immediately classified as top secret, and many in the government joked that NSA stood for "No Such Agency." The NSA's role is to collect and interpret foreign intelligence communications, to break foreign encryptions, and to protect American communication systems from outside networks. The NSA is overseen by and reports to the Department of Defense.

The role of the NSA is often confused with that of the CIA. While the latter gathers information internationally, NSA agents are based mostly in the United States. The type of information they gather is referred to as metadata. This includes such items as records of phone calls, emails, and social media posts.

Since 2001, the NSA has used a number of programs to deal with the flood of information that is sent via new technologies, such as texts and emails. This has led to many criticisms about whether the collection of such data is legal, or whether it oversteps the individual's right to privacy. This issue of national security versus personal privacy came to the forefront in the aftermath of Edward Snowden's document leaks.

The south tower of the World Trade Center in New York explodes after being hit by a hijacked plane on the morning of September 11, 2001.

What Led to Snowden's Actions?

Chapter Two

On September 11, 2001, the United States was forever changed. Millions of people around the world watched in horror as a terrorist attack unfolded on their television screens. The events that followed in the coming days and months would create the environment that drove Edward Snowden to blow the whistle.

At 8:45 a.m. on that busy Tuesday morning, people were arriving to work at the World Trade Center in New York City the same as they always did. Some had already been in their offices for hours, while others were preparing to start their day. Suddenly, a jet crashed into the side of the 110-story building. The plane had been hijacked while in flight. Just eighteen minutes later, another hijacked flight crashed into the second tower. A third flight crashed into the Pentagon, in Arlington, Virginia, shortly after. Another plane, believed to be aimed toward the Capitol Building, failed to reach its destination after passengers overwhelmed the hijackers and caused it to crash in Pennsylvania.

Horrified onlookers fled. Some leaped from the windows of the buildings, hoping to reach safety. The towers burned and eventually collapsed. While emergency teams worked around the clock to search for survivors, volunteers set up makeshift shelters and memorials. All flights across the United States were grounded for the remainder of the day and much of the next. The nation's skies took on an eerie silence, save for the US Air Force patrols over New York City and Washington, DC.

Almost three thousand people died in the attacks; more than six thousand were injured. It was the largest foreign attack on US soil. America and the world would never be the same again. At the time, the United States was not engaged in any wars. That would soon change.

There is a quote by Founding Father Benjamin Franklin that has been much repeated and paraphrased since 2001. The full version reads: "Those who would give up essential Liberty, to purchase a little temporary Safety, deserve neither Liberty nor Safety." Many people have speculated about its meaning over the past two decades. Some say that it is misused and misinterpreted, incorrectly being used to speak out against the loss of personal privacy. Others say just the opposite—that Franklin was warning about the sacrifice of privacy, or liberty, in the name of national security. To give up our personal

Computer networks stream much of the data that is used to conduct everyday business, from communications to banking.

liberties, so carefully protected by the Constitution, for the sake of broader safety results in the loss of both.

After the Attack

Events following the terrorist attacks on September 11 have raised many questions. If the government enacts laws such as those that allow for eavesdropping, but they are designed for the greater good, does that protect all citizens and make them safer? Does it ultimately give people greater freedom, or is a freer society only possible if individual rights are guaranteed and citizens can be safe in the knowledge that they are not being monitored? How much privacy can people really expect when so much of their personal information is available online and so much of our everyday business—banking, health care, and more—is stored in the virtual world?

Thousands of American troops have been deployed to the Middle East since 2001 as part of the war on terror.

As the nation mourned its losses following the devastating attacks, the US government was swift to react. Within a few days, President Bush spoke of the need for a war on terrorism. This was soon shortened to the war on terror. It began with the invasion of Afghanistan, with the intention of bringing down al-Qaeda and the ruling Taliban government. By March 2003, the war on terror expanded to Iraq, where a US-led invasion deposed President Saddam Hussein. The rationale behind the invasion was that Iraq was producing weapons of mass destruction (WMD), although none had ever been found. At the time of this writing, the war continues, making it the longest that the United States has been involved in. The military pulled out of Iraq in December 2011, leaving behind a volatile nation. As for Afghanistan, formal combat may have ended in 2014, but thousands of troops remain in the region. Al-Qaeda has fallen by the wayside, only to be replaced by the Islamic State of Iraq and Syria, better known as ISIS, Islamic State, or its Arabic name, Daesh.

Effects in the United States

The war on terror has had long-lasting effects throughout the Middle East. Although it has been a repeated claim that life continues as normal in the United States, and that terrorism has not been allowed to win, the truth is that multiple changes in security, surveillance, and personal privacy resulted from the September 11 attacks.

For example, one of the most marked differences is in air travel. Gone are the days of a simple security check and friends accompanying passengers to the gate to wave them off. Instead, a growing list of restrictions faces passengers. Before flying these days, passengers must remove jackets and shoes as well as laptops and all liquids from their carry-on bags. Next, they pass through full-body scanners and may also be required to undergo a pat-down. The Transportation Safety Administration (TSA), which was created as a result of the September 11 attacks, claims that this is necessary to guarantee safety on a flight. Critics argue that it invades personal freedom, leads to unfair targeting of some passengers based on ethnicity, and cannot be shown to have prevented any terrorist attacks.

Another example of a more serious human rights violation is the detention center at Guantanamo Bay in Cuba, which opened in 2002 to hold suspected enemy combatants. The inmate population rose to more than 650 within just one year. Many were held without access to legal counsel or a proper trial.

Many more changes have been hidden away, unknown to the average American. That is, until Edward Snowden decided that the public had a right to know.

In the months and years immediately following September 11, Congress dramatically increased budgetary spending in the name of national security. In 2002, President Bush created the Department of Homeland Security (DHS), charged with "preparing for and preventing domestic emergencies, especially terrorism." The DHS absorbed several existing agencies and now oversees immigration, customs, and border patrol. The Coast Guard, Secret Service, and Federal Emergency Management Agency (FEMA) also fall within its scope. Homeland Security's 2002 budget of $16 billion has increased to as much as $40 billion or more since 2011. The increased government spending is meant to cover more staff, more investigations, and more surveillance. As Snowden soon learned, after September 11, there was a boom in secret surveillance.

The NSA and Leaking

Since its formation during the Truman administration, the National Security Agency (NSA) has worked to intercept and decrypt coded foreign transmissions. They were limited to foreign communications. The Fourth Amendment to the US Constitution prohibits "unreasonable searches and seizures" against American citizens. In other words, the NSA could not conduct surveillance or gather information (metadata) from American citizens without probable cause and a court order permitting them to do so.

As far back as the 1960s, there were leaks and revelations that the NSA had overstepped its legal bounds by spying on American citizens. In 1962, the NSA began to keep a list of American citizens who had traveled to Cuba. The list later included those suspected of trafficking drugs. Despite being citizens and therefore being protected by the Constitution, the people on this list were unknowingly monitored. Their communications were intercepted and shared among various bureaus, including the CIA and the Federal Bureau of Investigation (FBI). In 1967, President Johnson added to the list the names of prominent activists who opposed the war in Vietnam. President Nixon expanded the program, known as Project Minaret, to include journalists, civil rights activists, and even some senators. There were no court orders or warrants permitting this surveillance. Among those included on Project Minaret's watch list: boxer Muhammad Ali, actress Jane Fonda, and civil rights leader Martin Luther King Jr. One other name on the list was Senator Frank Church.

Following several newspaper reports in the early 1970s that alluded to the agency's spying on its own citizens, a Senate committee was formed to investigate NSA activities. Church, a senator from Idaho, led this committee, commonly known as the Church Committee. At the time of the investigation, most of those on Capitol Hill had little idea

Anti–Vietnam War protesters were subject to secret NSA surveillance under Project Minaret.

what the NSA did. It was veiled in secrecy. Church and his colleagues were astonished to discover the extent of their surveillance programs, seemingly without any real oversight. Telephone calls, telegrams, and other communications were regularly monitored without judicial approval. Church warned that the NSA had the power "to impose total tyranny, and there would be no way to fight back." Despite the committee's findings, many criticized Church for limiting the powers of the CIA and NSA to do their jobs. In 1980, Church lost his bid for reelection. One of his opponent's main allegations was that Church had betrayed the intelligence agencies.

FISA

One positive result of the Church Committee's findings was the passing of the Foreign Intelligence Surveillance Act (FISA) in 1978. The act created a special FISA court that would make sure that Congress and the judicial system provided proper oversight of surveillance programs. At the same time, it ensured that national security was protected by keeping such programs out of the public eye. President Carter signed the act into law. Since its inception, the court has met in secret to approve or deny warrants for surveillance. No details are made public except for the total number of warrants approved each year. To provide some context for how the amount of surveillance has increased, in the court's first year (1980) 322 warrants were approved. By 2016, this number had grown to 1,401.

Through the 1980s and 1990s, FISA seemed to provide the correct amount of oversight. Things changed in 2001 as the war on terror launched. One question on people's minds was why the NSA failed to provide any warning that the terrorist attacks might happen. If they were monitoring and intercepting foreign communications, surely they must have found something. Perhaps they needed extra powers of surveillance. Thus began the weakening of the oversights.

A few years earlier, in 1999, the concept of contact chaining had been brought before the court for consideration. Contact chaining is the collection of various forms of metadata—phone numbers dialed, email addresses, and so on—and then providing a computer analysis of a person's movements and activities based upon that data. The analysis then searches for other people whose data overlaps, thereby creating a social map of communications between people without ever listening to a single phone call or reading an email. The Justice Department ruled that contact chaining as a means of surveillance was not permissible on American citizens, nor on any transmissions passing through the United States.

Tackling Surveillance and Privacy

Nearly two decades later, the nation's courts continue to struggle with how to balance privacy with security when it comes to new technologies. Advances in how business is conducted, communication, and how data is stored have moved faster than the laws that govern them. For example, at what point is a warrant required to obtain data? In 1979, the Supreme Court ruled that there was no expectation of privacy when making a telephone call because the number dialed was given to a third party—a telephone company. In the 1980s, the Stored Communications Act laid out strict guidelines to be followed before a service provider could be ordered to hand over customers' private information. This was during the earliest days of the internet and cell phone usage. Since then, usage of both has ballooned, and so have the issues related to privacy. In 2014, the Supreme Court decided that an individual's cell phone was covered by the Fourth Amendment. In other words, seizure of a person's cell phone and the inspection of its data without a warrant was an unreasonable search. In 2017, the issue reached the Supreme Court once again, as *Carpenter v. United States* challenged the right of any government agency to obtain location data from a cell phone–service provider without a warrant. The data in question is cell phone location-tracking data. Such data tracking is an integral part of contact chaining. Does gathering it constitute a breach of personal privacy? While this particular case is related to a criminal investigation, one can take it further to ask: What if this were for a national security investigation? Would it still be a breach of privacy?

Back in 2001, after September 11, arguments of personal privacy were overruled by matters of national security. There was a clamor for answers and solutions, and if that meant changing the rules of what was permitted, so be it. At the time, some of the changes were done without Congressional knowledge. On October 4, 2001, Project Stellar Wind began operation with no court approval. The program, so secret that most people within the NSA and Congress would not know about it until the following year, used contact chaining as a means of gathering as much surveillance data as possible, on both foreigners and American citizens. Stellar Wind was exposed to the American public in the *New York Times* in 2008.

Also in October came the signing into law of the Uniting and Strengthening America by Providing Appropriate Tools Required to Intercept and Obstruct Terrorism Act of 2001, better known as the USA PATRIOT Act, or simply the Patriot Act. Given the immense sense of shock that an attack could (and did) take place on American soil, support for the Patriot Act was overwhelming. Only one senator voted against it. In the House of Representatives, it passed with 357 to 66 votes. One of those who opposed the act was libertarian Ron Paul, who argued vehemently that it overrode too many constitutionally protected rights to privacy. The American Civil Liberties Union (ACLU) also voiced its concerns about the Patriot Act, arguing that it had been passed too quickly, without proper consideration. On the organization's website is the following statement:

The Patriot Act was the first of many changes to surveillance laws that made it easier for the government to spy on ordinary Americans by expanding the authority to monitor phone and email communications, collect bank and credit reporting records, and track the activity of innocent Americans on the Internet. While most Americans think it was created to catch terrorists, the Patriot Act actually turns regular citizens into suspects.

The ACLU argued that much of the Patriot Act was in violation of the Fourth Amendment to the Constitution, governing proper search and seizure. Among the provisions of the Patriot Act were: permission for law enforcement to search homes or businesses without the owner's knowledge or consent; expanded permission for the FBI to search various records without a warrant; and indefinite detention of suspected enemy combatants without trial.

William Binney

Just a few days after the passage of the Patriot Act, a senior NSA analyst named William Binney resigned from the NSA. He went on to become an outspoken critic of their surveillance activities, and he no doubt served as an inspiration for Edward Snowden many years later.

Binney was a cryptomathematician with the NSA. For many years, he had worked on decrypting communications related to Cold War threats. The 1990s saw a move away from Eastern Europe and toward the quickly developing technology of the internet. The internet not only changed methods of communication, it also changed how data could be gathered and interpreted. Binney and his colleagues developed ways to automate the analysis of metadata, vastly speeding up the process of gathering and interpreting. Binney stated that he had several grievances with the NSA. First, he was infuriated that the agency had not prevented the September 11 attacks. He later claimed that they had failed to analyze data that would have revealed the terrorist plot in a timely manner. Second, he was opposed to Stellar Wind and the widespread eavesdropping on American citizens without a warrant. He claims that the decision to spy on Americans was made within a week of the attacks and that the NSA wanted information on everyone and everything. After attempting to utilize the agency's internal whistle-blower program to express his concerns, Binney felt that he had no choice but to resign. Over the next few years, Binney was investigated and his property confiscated. Not until 2012 would a court finally order his property to be returned. Edward Snowden would later decide to make his revelations in the manner he did—to the press, rather than through existing internal whistle-blower programs—in large part as a result of how Binney and others like him had been treated. He believed that the whistle-blower program was little more than theater.

In 2002, Binney asked the inspector general of the Department of Defense to investigate some of the NSA programs. This is when Congress learned, for the first time, about the new sweeping methods of data collection. Despite surprise at such a revelation, the general feeling seemed to have reflected the idea that some privacy intrusions were acceptable if they were important to national security.

Telling the Public

The first real leaks to the American public about the NSA's expanded powers came in late 2005. A headline in the *New York Times* read: "Bush Lets U.S. Spy on Callers Without Courts." The story told how, in the months immediately following September 11, President Bush gave authorization for NSA eavesdropping within the United States in the hunt for evidence of terrorist plots, and that this authorization allowed them to do so without warrants. In addition to including the concerns of critics (such as Binney) that the program overstepped constitutional limits, the authors of the story noted: "Defenders of the program say it has been a critical tool in helping disrupt terrorist plots and prevent attacks inside the United States." Although the article mentioned the interception of communications without warrants, it did not reveal the extent to which metadata was being collected.

A Barrage of Bills and Secrets

In 2006, several bills related to electronic surveillance and the authorization of such surveillance were introduced in Congress. The proposed Terrorist Surveillance Act would give the president additional authority to carry on surveillance of suspected terrorists within the United States. There would be Congressional oversight of such surveillance. The proposed

National Security Surveillance Act would amend FISA, granting amnesty for previous surveillance that had been carried out without a warrant if it had been authorized by the president. Meanwhile, the proposed Foreign Intelligence Surveillance Improvement and Enhancement Act would allow FISA the sole authority to conduct electronic foreign surveillance. All were sent to the Senate for further discussion, but none were passed.

During that same session, another bill was proposed: the Electronic Surveillance Modernization Act, which would allow the president to authorize surveillance of international phone calls as well as email that could be linked to terrorist groups. This, too, was sent to the Senate, but never passed.

Matters of electronic surveillance were on the minds of those in Washington. Such legislation raised many questions related to privacy and national security. At what point did one overrule the other? Civil liberties organizations and constitutional scholars became even more vocal about the issue in 2007. President Bush signed into law the Protect America Act of 2007. This amendment to FISA removed all need for a judicial warrant when spying on foreign intelligence targets who were "reasonably believed" to be located outside the United States.

One year later, President Bush signed the FISA Amendments Act (FAA). In effect, this gave official approval to what the NSA had already been doing for years. The amount of time during which surveillance could be carried out without a warrant increased, and special provisions were enacted to enable eavesdropping in an emergency.

President George W. Bush signed the FISA Amendments Act in 2008, increasing NSA powers regarding electronic surveillance.

One particular point of interest was the vote of the future president, Senator Barack Obama of Illinois. In 2006, he spoke out against the appointment of Michael Hayden as CIA director, saying, "We need to find a way forward to make sure that we can stop terrorists while protecting the privacy, and liberty, of innocent Americans." He warned about the dangers of surveillance going too far without proper oversight. He frequently criticized warrantless wiretaps. In 2008, Senator Obama voted in favor of the FAA. When faced with criticism from supporters and the media, he claimed that the bill was an "improvement" over the Protect America Act and that it provided "appropriate safeguards."

Later in 2008, Obama won the presidential election. In October 2012, shortly before being elected to a second term in office, he signed Presidential Policy Directive 20. The directive's content remained secret and unknown until Edward Snowden revealed it in 2013. The document was said to be a framework for US cybersecurity by establishing principles and processes. The *Washington Post* reported that it "enables the military to act more aggressively to thwart cyberattacks on the nation's web of government and private computer networks."

The decades-old nickname for the NSA, "No Such Agency," took on a new meaning in 2012. Journalist James Bamford suggested that it now stood for "Never Say Anything." Bamford wrote in *Wired* magazine that the NSA was building a giant, top-secret, data collection center in remote Utah. The center would provide "near-bottomless" storage for the mass collection of private data. In the following weeks, the NSA's director, General Keith

Alexander, was asked by Congress about the story and about the agency's capabilities. Alexander repeatedly denied that the NSA was engaged in spying on American citizens through data (emails, telephone calls, etc.). He also claimed that they did not have the technical capabilities to do so. Such data collection, he reasoned, would not be possible without a warrant. Furthermore, it would fall under the jurisdiction of the FBI rather than the NSA.

Director of National Intelligence James Clapper reiterated Alexander's claims in March 2013. Testifying before a Senate panel, he said that the NSA did not spy on American citizens. He went on to explain that any mass data collection did not happen "wittingly," but could have been inadvertently gathered while eavesdropping on foreign suspects.

Within a matter of months, Clapper's statements and those of many others would be called into question, as document after document was leaked to the global press. When questioned again, Clapper claimed he had not thought about the Patriot Act and data collection because the program was classified.

Timeline of Events

1952 Formation of the National Security Agency.

1978 Foreign Intelligence Surveillance Act is signed into law.

1999 US Justice Department rules that contact chaining is not permissible on US citizens.

2001 Terrorist attacks occur against the World Trade Center in New York and the Pentagon in Virginia.

2001 Project Stellar Wind begins operation. Invasion of Afghanistan launches the war on terror. USA PATRIOT ACT is signed into law.

2002 Department of Homeland Security is formed.

2007 Protect America Act is signed into law.

2008 FISA Amendments Act is signed into law.

2012 The NSA director denies that the agency is involved in spying on American citizens or is monitoring electronic communications.

2012 Presidential Policy Directive 20 is signed in secret by President Obama.

2013 National Intelligence Director denies that the NSA engages in collection of metadata from American citizens.

2013 The *Guardian* publishes the first in a series of stories based upon documents leaked by Edward Snowden; Snowden is revealed as the source behind the stories in the *Guardian* and the *Washington Post*.

On May 29, 2017, Edward Snowden gave an interview from Moscow discussing surveillance of citizens in Japan.

Snowden's Leaks

To many people, a career in intelligence conjures up images of international spies leading glamorous lives as they trot the globe, going from one dangerous adventure to the next. If that were the case, Edward Joseph Snowden would be possibly the last person who might fit such a stereotype.

The reality is that a large portion of intelligence work is carried out by highly educated and skilled technical experts. They spend their days staring at computer screens and analyzing data. Snowden would fit this image much more closely. Even then, there is still one important difference. Edward Snowden was not highly educated, at least not in the traditional sense. He did not have a graduate degree, nor an undergraduate degree. In fact, he didn't even graduate from high school.

Snowden seemed to have stopped going to school when he was just fifteen. He has claimed that a prolonged bout of strep throat kept him out of school for nine months, but some journalists say that his school records show no indication of such illness. He simply stopped attending. He was born in North Carolina, and he and his family moved to Maryland in the early 1990s, where his father was a Coast Guard officer and his mother worked in the US District Court. His parents split up while Edward was a teenager. Since he was not attending school, much of his time was spent in his room. He had bought a computer and would spend hours online socializing in chat rooms and teaching himself programming. He eventually completed his GED through the local community college. Snowden claims to have studied Japanese and to have taken some university classes, although there seems to be little proof of either, and he never earned a college degree of any sort.

Military Service and the CIA

The records of his online chats during this time and in the coming years would later provide a fascinating glimpse into Edward Snowden's character. A proud patriot, he was a proponent of gun ownership and a supporter of libertarian Ron Paul's presidential campaign. He expressed a desire to fight in the Iraq war because "I felt like I had an obligation as a human being to help free people from oppression."

Keen to follow in the footsteps of his father and grandfather, who were both in the military, Snowden enlisted in the US Army Reserves in 2004. He entered through a special enlistment program that would allow him to try out for the Special Forces during his training. Like his education, his military training was never completed. Again, reasons vary. Chat room records from the time indicate that he simply "washed out," and he received an administrative discharge. Later, Snowden would claim that he broke both legs and was unable to continue. There seems to be no record of a medical discharge. He also found himself disappointed in his fellow recruits, many of whom "seemed pumped up about killing Arabs" rather than fighting for justice and helping others.

In 2006, Snowden got a job at the CIA's global communications division after a brief period working as a security guard. He did not have a college degree, which the agency's website lists as a minimum requirement for an intelligence analyst position. His grandfather was a rear admiral in the US Coast Guard who worked in the FBI after retirement from the military. Did his grandfather's influence help him get the job?

Snowden spent some time in Geneva in 2007, working on computer network security. Reports of his exact role here differ. Officials say that he provided technical support and little else. Snowden claims this time was spent developing his spy training. He says he became disillusioned after watching American intelligence colleagues manipulate and blackmail people into providing information. Whatever the truth, Snowden enjoyed the benefits of a six-month overseas posting with a good income and a very comfortable lifestyle.

Leaving Langley and Dell

After that posting, he was sent back to headquarters in Langley, Virginia. In February 2009, he abruptly resigned. Some journalists have speculated that his behavior at work had resulted in a negative evaluation. It is also believed that he resigned to avoid an internal investigation. He immediately took a position with the Dell computer company in Japan. Dell completed contracts for the NSA, and Snowden's CIA experience and security clearance made him an excellent candidate for their Tokyo facility. While there, his job was to show the military and government offices how to defend their computer networks from potential hackers.

After returning to Maryland in 2011 and spending a year as a technician with Dell on their CIA accounts, he relocated again. This time, he and his girlfriend moved to Hawaii. Still an employee of Dell, Snowden was now posted at the NSA's regional operations center on the island paradise of Kauai. Here, as in his earlier life, Snowden was rather introverted. He preferred to spend his time chatting online under an alias rather than in the company of work colleagues or friends.

Whistle-Blowing

Snowden left his position at Dell in 2013, moving to Booz Allen Hamilton, another NSA subcontractor. His work at Dell had given him access to top-secret NSA materials. His new position provided access to different documents. This is why, he later disclosed, he had sought employment there. "My position with Booz Allen Hamilton granted me access to lists of machines all over the world the NSA hacked,"

The house in Hawaii where Edward Snowden lived with his girlfriend before he flew to Hong Kong in May 2013

Snowden said. "That is why I accepted that position." On his application, Snowden claimed that he was about to earn a graduate degree. This was a fabrication, but one that was apparently overlooked. Nevertheless, his time at Booz Allen Hamilton would be short-lived. On May 20, 2013, Snowden called into work to say that he was undergoing tests for epilepsy and would be taking some time off. Leaving a brief note for his girlfriend explaining that he was going on a business trip, he boarded a plane for Hong Kong.

As Snowden left Hawaii, neither his girlfriend nor his work colleagues had any reason to suspect anything out of the ordinary. Little did they know that for several months he had been attempting to make contact with leading political journalist Glenn Greenwald and independent filmmaker Laura Poitras. He was planning to meet them in Hong Kong so that he might share his secrets.

Reporter Glenn Greenwald, a former lawyer, was contacted by Edward Snowden and flew to meet him in Hong Kong.

Glenn Greenwald left a decade-long career as a constitutional lawyer and turned to political journalism in the mid-2000s. As a blogger and writer for *Salon*, he frequently wrote about issues related to the intelligence community, including CIA investigations and allegations of NSA eavesdropping without warrants. In the summer of 2012, he left *Salon* and took a position at the *Guardian*.

In December of the same year, at his home in Brazil, he received an email from an anonymous source. The source said that he had important documents to share and requested his encryption key. Such a key would allow for the private exchange of coded emails and protection from possible prying eyes. Greenwald, by his own admission, did not have one. Although the nature of his work regularly involved sensitive material, he was not a particularly tech-savvy person. Since the email gave no other information, he ignored it. He ignored several further attempts at contact, in which the source sent detailed instructions for how to set up an encryption key. Little did he know that the sender of the email would be the biggest news story of his career.

Laura Poitras, an award-winning independent filmmaker, had received an Academy Award nomination for her 2006 film, *My Country, My Country*, which explored what it was like for Iraqis to live under US occupation. In 2010, she made *The Oath*, about a couple of Yemeni men and their legal battles during the war on terror. The documentary won an award for excellence in cinematography at the Sundance Film Festival. As a result of her work, she was subject to frequent surveillance by US authorities. She moved to Berlin for several years to protect her work and her privacy.

Filmmaker Laura Poitras flew to Hong Kong with Greenwald. Her documentary *Citizenfour* tells the story of Edward Snowden.

In January 2013, she received the first of many encrypted emails. Unlike Greenwald, she was used to encryption methods and was able to carry out a correspondence with the source, who used the signature Citizenfour. As the two communicated, Citizenfour explained that he had a number of sensitive documents he wished to reveal. He also wanted her to reach out to Greenwald and suggest they work together. His attempts to contact Greenwald had proven unsuccessful, and he thought that she might have better luck in convincing him that this was a lead worth pursuing. The anonymous sender of the emails told her that he wanted his identity to eventually become known in case remaining hidden put his loved ones at risk.

Poitras was intrigued. The communications were consistent enough that she believed Citizenfour was genuine. She made contact with Greenwald, who adopted the necessary encryption methods. The two began communicating with Citizenfour. In May, he told them that they should meet in person in Hong Kong.

The filmmaker and the journalist both traveled to New York first, where they met with the US editor of the *Guardian*. It was decided that they should both travel to Hong Kong, and that they should be accompanied by Ewen MacAskill, the *Guardian*'s intelligence correspondent.

Plans to meet in Hong Kong mirrored those in any James Bond movie. Citizenfour sent careful instructions that they were to wait outside a specific restaurant at a specific time. He would be there. They would be able to identify him by the Rubik's Cube he would carry.

Greenwald and Poitras went to the planned rendezvous point. It had been agreed that MacAskill would join them the next day, so as not to panic the source. Given the amount and high levels of information that the source claimed to have, both were expecting the mysterious source to be a grizzled government worker, jaded after twenty or thirty years of intelligence work. Neither was prepared for the boyish-looking man in glasses and a T-shirt carrying the all-important Rubik's Cube. As he walked past, he gave them instructions to follow him to the nearby Hotel Mira.

Over the next few days, Greenwald, Poitras, and MacAskill met with Snowden in his cramped hotel room.

Far below were the bustling streets of Hong Kong, but here, Snowden spent his days in isolation with only the television and his laptop for company. He claimed to have not been outside since his arrival at the hotel. Poitras filmed much of their time together; it would form the core of her future award-winning documentary, *Citizenfour*. Snowden took exceptional measures to ensure they were not being listened to as they chatted. He unplugged the phone, placed pillows at the bottom of the room's door, and urged extreme caution with the use of cell phones or laptops. He showed Greenwald how to protect and encrypt the stories he sent to his editors, and he hid beneath a cloak when entering passwords into his own computer.

What Was Said

One of the first questions MacAskill had for him was simple: What is your name? Despite several months of communication (in Poitras's case), they still did not know his name or anything about him. As they chatted about his background, Snowden expressed concern about the media focus on personalities. He wanted the story to be the information he was leaking, not himself. He felt that to focus on him would distract from the real point of his actions: to let people know about the unauthorized collection of data about millions of everyday Americans. Snowden would frequently repeat, "I am not the story."

As can be seen in Poitras's documentary, Snowden talked to them about what he believed to be the false promises of the US government. He said that Barack Obama had promised, when running for election, that he would reduce the number of drone strikes and limit invasions of privacy. After winning the presidency, Snowden said, Obama had failed to keep his promises, instead increasing strikes. A June 27 story by Greenwald showed that President Obama had also continued to allow the bulk collection of emails under the Stellar Wind program for two years after taking office. Snowden mourned the loss of personal privacy and liberty. He spoke of how it is now commonplace for people to joke that they are "on the list" or under surveillance, often only half-aware of just how much their moves are being monitored. This loss of privacy and personal liberty, he argues, not only goes against the Constitution, but limits "the boundaries of intellectual expansion." If people are afraid that they are being tracked, they become less willing to express opinions and to exchange ideas. He decided to leak the documents he had stolen to provide people with knowledge. With knowledge, they could "meaningfully oppose state power."

Going into more detail about the NSA's surveillance methods, Snowden said that the agency worked with foreign governments and other intelligence agencies to create a framework capable of intercepting every piece of digital, radio, or analog data that is transmitted. In addition to implicating the NSA and the US government, Snowden also leaked a great deal of information related to GCHQ, the British intelligence organization.

During their time together, Snowden provided Poitras and Greenwald with thousands of classified documents. Why did he approach the press rather than follow agency

Filipino refugee Vanessa
Rodel was one of several
who helped to shelter
Edward Snowden during
his time in Hong Kong.

procedures that were in place for whistle-blowers? Snowden expressed a lack of trust, particularly considering how previous whistle-blowers such as William Binney and Chelsea Manning had been treated. How could he be treated fairly, he reasoned, if the only people he could bring his concerns to were his superiors, responsible for the very actions he was concerned about? At the same time, he did not feel that he alone should hold this amount of information and be responsible for what the public knew. By giving the information to Greenwald and Poitras, he said that he was giving others the opportunity to decide what should be made available.

The *Guardian* Article and Aftermath

On June 6, 2013, the *Guardian* ran Greenwald's story with the headline mentioned earlier: "NSA Collecting Phone Records of Millions of Verizon Customers Daily." In the story, Greenwald explained the extent of the metadata collection and shared a copy of the court order permitting the action. Within hours, the story was being broadcast around the world. This was just the beginning. Before the year was out, the *Guardian* would run more than two hundred additional stories on the topic. The next day, the *Washington Post* ran a related story by Laura Poitras and journalist Barton Gellman with the headline "U.S., British Intelligence

Mining Data from Nine U.S. Internet Companies in Broad Secret Program." While the cable news networks broadcast little else over the next few days, stories also appeared elsewhere. *Le Monde*, *Der Spiegel*, the *New York Times*, and countless other outlets all speculated on what this meant, and who was behind the leaks.

As had been previously decided, the first stories gave no hint as to Snowden's identity. The focus was on the shocking levels of surveillance rather than the person behind the revelations. The secret could not be kept indefinitely, however. Snowden had always said that he planned to make himself known. He knew that continuing to remain anonymous could endanger his girlfriend or his family, none of whom knew where he was or what he had done. Within a day or two of the first story breaking, NSA agents had been to his house in Hawaii to look for him. Although he felt confident that they were asking just out of routine because of his extended sick leave, he and the journalists debated when he should go public. He decided it should be sooner rather than later.

On June 9, a video appeared on the *Guardian*'s website. It identified Snowden as the NSA whistle-blower, as he stated: "I don't want to live in a society that does these sorts of things." On June 11, a story jointly authored by Greenwald, Poitras, and MacAskill gave more information about Snowden. He explained his reasons for making the documents public and reiterated that he never planned to stay anonymous. He also expressed uncertainty over what would happen to him next.

Once Snowden's identity was revealed to the world, it didn't take long for the media to track him down to Hong Kong and to the Hotel Mira. The decision was made to change location. Greenwald and Poitras left the city. Meanwhile, Snowden went into hiding and began making plans for his future. He applied to the United Nations for refugee status, and it was later discovered that he spent the following days in a tiny apartment with other refugees and asylum-seekers.

While seeking refugee status, Snowden reportedly began approaching countries that might be willing to protect him from extradition to the United States. The question of asylum is interesting. For starters, many refugees spend years, even decades, waiting for their cases to be considered. Furthermore, the office of the United Nations High Commission for Refugees said that if he did apply, there would be no reason why his application should be fast-tracked. At the same time, only two countries accept refugees from Hong Kong, and those are the United States and Canada. Why would he apply for such a status, if indeed he did?

There is also the matter of whether Snowden's circumstances would qualify him for refugee status, wherever he happened to be at the time of application. Many legal scholars said no. According to the United Nations' definition of a refugee, Snowden would have to make the case that he risked being persecuted for his political opinion, and that the crimes he was charged with were not political. On June 21, 2013, the US Department of Justice filed several charges against him, including violation of the Espionage Act of 1917 and theft of government property. Lawyers have argued that he faced prosecution not for his political opinion but for violating US law, namely by committing espionage and theft.

Finding Refuge in Others

At some point, WikiLeaks founder Julian Assange took up Snowden's cause and became involved. Assange had established WikiLeaks in 2006, but it gained attention in 2010, when the site released information provided by whistle-blower Chelsea Manning.

As an intelligence analyst in the US Army, Manning had access to classified information related to the Iraq and Afghanistan Wars and downloaded thousands of documents. When several newspapers showed no interest, Manning posted some of the information on the WikiLeaks site. Among the information leaked was video footage of US soldiers committing executions and congratulating themselves for having killed people during an attack on Baghdad. Following a court-martial, Manning was sentenced to thirty-five years in prison. In 2016, shortly before leaving office, President Obama commuted her sentence to time served.

Back in 2010, when Manning's leaks were first shared, Snowden had expressed his dislike of WikiLeaks in online chat rooms. His views apparently changed over time. Assange could not travel since he has lived in London's Ecuadorian Embassy since 2012, avoiding his own extradition. However, he sent his assistant to Hong Kong to help broker an asylum deal.

From Hong Kong to Russia

After criminal charges were filed against Snowden, the United States requested that the Hong Kong government extradite him so that he might face trial. The following day, his passport was reportedly canceled. In theory, this should have rendered him unable to leave Hong Kong for any destination except a return to the United States.

On June 23, Edward Snowden boarded an Aeroflot flight to Moscow, accompanied by Assange's assistant. Some reports claim that he had stayed at the Russian Embassy in Hong Kong the previous night and had already decided to seek asylum in Russia. Venezuela, Ecuador, Nicaragua, and Bolivia had made offers to Snowden, saying that they would welcome him. He was unable to take a flight that passed through the United States, however. He also feared that any flight passing through a European capital would prove unsafe. The latter fear proved to be well founded after a flight carrying the Bolivian president was diverted, forced to land in Vienna, and searched in case it might be transporting Snowden.

Upon arrival in Moscow, Snowden was denied entry on the grounds that his passport was no longer valid. This raises the question of how he was able to board a flight out of Hong Kong in the first place. Various reasons have been offered, including a glitch in paperwork causing a delay in his passport's cancelation, and the intervention of Vladimir Putin, who was keen to get him onto Russian soil. For the next month, the whistle-blower took residence in the transit lounge at Moscow's Sheremetyevo International Airport. He

A plane lands at Moscow's Sheremetyevo Airport. Snowden spent over a month in the transit zone in 2013 while he applied for asylum.

Ewen MacAskill

Edward Snowden personally reached out to Glenn Greenwald and Laura Poitras, but why was Ewen MacAskill chosen to accompany them to Hong Kong?

MacAskill is a Scottish journalist. He began his career as political editor at the *Scotsman*, an Edinburgh-based daily newspaper, in 1990. After six years there, he became the chief political correspondent for the *Guardian*, and then the newspaper's diplomatic editor. In 2007, the *Guardian* asked him to head their news bureau in Washington, DC. It was while he was in the United States that Snowden approached Greenwald. Greenwald contacted his editor, who in turn contacted MacAskill. Poitras recommended that MacAskill accompany Greenwald to Hong Kong. If this story was truly going to be as explosive as they suspected, it would be important to have an experienced bureau chief there.

At first, Poitras was unhappy about his presence on the trip to Hong Kong. She feared that Snowden would cancel the meeting when he saw a third party. It was decided that she and Greenwald alone would meet the whistle-blower at the planned rendezvous point. MacAskill joined them at the hotel the following day, once Snowden had given his approval. Since then, MacAskill has met with Snowden several times in Moscow. He calls Snowden "the perfect source" and says that he enjoys "relative freedom in exile."

held a press conference for a few carefully selected members of human rights organizations on July 12, where he released a statement, part of which read:

> I did not seek to enrich myself. I did not seek to sell US secrets. I did not partner with any foreign government to guarantee my safety. Instead, I took what I knew to the public, so what affects all of us can be discussed by all of us in the light of day, and I asked the world for justice. That moral decision to tell the public about spying that affects all of us has been costly, but it was the right thing to do and I have no regrets.

He went on to thank those countries that had offered to help him, even in the face of "historically disproportionate aggression" from the United States. He said that while he accepted the offers of asylum from Latin America, it would currently be unsafe for him to travel there. For that reason, he formally requested asylum in Russia.

Snowden was granted asylum for one year. This has since been extended several times, currently allowing him to remain in Russia until at least 2020. He lives in an undisclosed location in Moscow with his girlfriend.

Questions Unanswered

Just how many documents Edward Snowden acquired may never be known. According to a later report by the House Permanent Select Committee on Intelligence, the number may be as high as 1.5 million. The report stated that what he gave to the journalists was merely a fraction of his entire haul. Intelligence agencies argued that documents he stole had the potential to endanger US troops and operatives in foreign countries and compromise the war on terror. Some documents that were revealed muddied international waters. For example, the world would soon learn that the NSA had been monitoring the private phone of Angela Merkel, the German chancellor. This raised questions on both sides of the spectrum. Why was the United States spying on its allies? What was Snowden's purpose in making such information known?

Perhaps the greatest ongoing concern is whether Snowden is also sharing the material that he stole with Russian intelligence. If so, how much? When his identity became known, many first suspected him of spying for or selling secrets to the Chinese. After all, he had chosen to fly to Hong Kong instead of any other destination. Once he settled in Russia, his motives were again challenged. Had he been planning a move to Moscow all along?

Jane Mayer interviews Snowden in 2014 at the New Yorker Festival.

Edward Snowden: Hero or Villain

Since Edward Snowden was first identified as the source of the leaks in the *Guardian* and the *Washington Post*, a fierce debate has raged about his intentions. It continues to this day. Is he a hero and a patriot who wanted to genuinely bring attention to what he saw as wrongdoing, who has now found himself trapped in a life of exile in Russia? Is he a villain and a traitor who turned his back on his country and the oath he swore to it, seeking to endanger the lives of many and weaken the international position of the United States? Did he seek monetary gain as a spy for China or Russia? Or is the truth somewhere in between?

To the three journalists who met with him in Hong Kong, Snowden was more than just a source. He was a truth-teller. Glenn Greenwald would later say that

Snowden seemed to see himself as the archetypal video game hero, "an ordinary individual who sees some serious injustice" and who decides it's up to him to right the wrong:

> It's all about figuring out ways to empower yourself as an ordinary person, to take on powerful forces in a way that allows you to undermine them in pursuit of some public good. Even if it's really risky or dangerous. That moral narrative at the heart of video games was part of his preadolescence and formed part of his moral understanding of the world and one's obligation as an individual.

Ewen MacAskill called Snowden "the perfect source." He described him as "self-effacing, motivated neither by money nor fame." It was these qualities that have made it hard for governments to demonize him, MacAskill has argued. After all, it is much easier to discredit someone if you can make the case that their actions were politically or financially driven. When someone has acted to correct what they see as a wrong against the American people, it is much harder to depict them as a villain.

Meanwhile, Laura Poitras criticized what she saw as a double standard within the American political and legal systems. She referred to General David Petraeus, the CIA director who had resigned in 2012 after it was revealed that he had been sharing classified information with his lover, a writer. Petraeus was given a short probationary sentence. Poitras compared this to the lengthy jail sentence that

Snowden would no doubt face if he returned to the United States, saying it was shameful to mistreat "whistle-blowers who do things as an act of conscience." She said that she believes Snowden "did something that he felt was to benefit not just US citizens but citizens all over the world."

What Is a Whistle-Blower?

Snowden and his supporters have always described his actions as those of a whistle-blower. What exactly is a whistle-blower, and what legal protections are in place for those who decide to spill secrets for the greater good?

Many believe that the term originated in the 1970s with environmental activist Ralph Nader, and that it refers to a sports referee who blows the whistle to call attention to a foul. In actuality, the term had already been in existence for at least a hundred years by then, and whistles have been historically used for centuries to alert communities or people to an event. The modern sports analogy is convenient but merely coincidental.

A whistle-blower is someone who exposes illegal or unethical wrongdoings, often by an employer or a larger organization. Such wrongdoings could include a contractor knowingly selling faulty equipment, a hospital committing insurance fraud, or a pharmaceutical company dumping illegal waste. Whistle-blowers do not always reveal wrongdoing within the government. Frank Serpico was a police officer who tried to expose corruption in the New York City police force in the 1970s. Karen Silkwood drew attention to health and safety issues at the nuclear facility where she worked.

Sherron Watkins is one of many who have become whistle-blowers to expose wrongdoings within their workplace.

Sherron Watkins exposed massive fraud at the financial company Enron. All made the decision to reveal what they considered unethical behaviors. When national security is the topic at hand, the question of what is unethical is often a personal decision. This can sometimes make the issue murkier. Are unethical actions sometimes necessary for the greater good? If so, who gets to define what that greater good is?

There are various ways for a whistle-blower to take action, and many organizations now have internal programs in place, supposedly to encourage people to speak out when they feel uncomfortable about a course of action. Technically, these programs protect a person from being fired or demoted after they have lodged a concern. In practice, though, this is often not the reality. Someone may be complaining about an unethical action to the very person doing the action. Are they really protected from retaliation in the workplace? Will anything be done as a result of their taking action? This is why an increasing number of whistle-blowers, such as Snowden, see these programs as ineffective and why they instead choose another route, either going to the press or leaking information online. Doing so often opens them up to criminal charges and prison time.

Laws About Whistle-Blowing

The very first whistle-blower law (the False Claims Act, or FCA) was enacted in 1863. Its goal was to encourage people to speak out against those who were defrauding the government during the Civil War. The law is still in place, albeit with various modifications. In 1912, the

Lloyd-La Follette Act was signed into law, specifically protecting federal employees and granting them the right to refer concerns to Congress without having to seek approval from their superiors. Nevertheless, the legal status of whistle-blowers remains rather vague. It raises questions of whether the revelations can ever be justified. Are there alternative methods of action? How harmful is the information that has been leaked, and to whom is it harmful?

In many cases of government whistle-blowing, protections are even more complicated. If issues related to national security are leaked, the person may be charged under the Espionage Act, as happened with both Edward Snowden and Chelsea Manning. The latter was sentenced to thirty-five years in prison for disclosing classified information, although the sentence was later commuted to seven years.

The National Whistleblower Center (NWC) and some experts says that all too often national security is used as an invalid argument. In an op-ed in the *Washington Post*, media historian Mark Feldstein said "Of course, some leaks—such as pending troop movements in wartime—can pose legitimate threats to national security. But political security—the covering-up of blunders and crimes by our leaders—has too often been the real reason for condemning leakers." He argues that whistle-blowing is "as American as apple pie" and says that it is a healthy part of any democracy.

Many government whistle-blowers have said that Snowden was right to do what he did in the way that he did. William Binney, Thomas Drake, and J. Kirk Wiebe are three of the four NSA whistle-blowers who, in 2002,

Chelsea Manning was court-martialed in 2013 for violating the Espionage Act. Her thirty-five-year sentence was later commuted to seven years by President Barack Obama.

asked the Department of Defense (DoD) to investigate the Trailblazer program. They argued that the failed data collection program was being mismanaged and had wasted millions of dollars, while a program that Binney had helped design would have cost less and, they claim, prevented the 9/11 attacks. All faced various forms of retaliation over many years, including armed FBI raids of their homes and seizure of personal property. Speaking to *USA Today* in 2013, shortly after Snowden's identity was revealed, the trio said that his leaks proved that they had been right all along. Telling reporters that Snowden's decision to go public was the right thing, Binney said that he had tried to remedy things "the right way" internally for seven years:

> We tried … to get the government to recognize the unconstitutional, illegal activity that they were doing and openly admit that … And that just failed totally because no one in Congress or—we couldn't get anybody in the courts, and certainly the Department of Justice and inspector general's office didn't pay any attention to it. And all of the efforts we made just produced no change whatsoever.

The three whistle-blowers expressed their frustration at how going through the official channels not only failed to produce any positive change but also resulted in negative impacts on them. Binney said that Snowden did "a really great public service" by bringing the issues of contact chaining and data collection into the public awareness. By doing so, he was forcing the government to be accountable. Thomas Drake was a former NSA executive who provided source information for the DoD investigation into Trailblazer and who later faced espionage charges for his actions. All charges were eventually dropped. Drake called Snowden "the classic whistleblower" whose actions were now forcing a debate about privacy and national security, a debate that he says should have occurred after the September 11 attacks. Drake has also spoken out against the growing trend towards prosecuting whistle-blowers, saying, "This makes a mockery of the entire classification system, where political gain is now incentive for leaking and whistleblowing is incentive for prosecution."

Honest Actions?

There were some reservations about Snowden's actions. Binney went on to express fears that Snowden was now transitioning from being a hero to being a traitor. Snowden had told the media that the United States had been hacking China and other foreign governments. To Binney, this went beyond his original claims of public service and seemed intended to do little but damage international relations. It would also give Snowden's opponents further ammunition to the argument that he was working for the Chinese or Russians. As one journalist would later write: "What Snowden exposed about the NSA's actions, as directed towards Americans, was both laudable, and badly needed. However, his leaks about American surveillance activities abroad, was misguided, and somewhat blind to the realities of today's geopolitical environment."

THE SECRET HISTORY
OF THE VIETNAM WAR

THE COMPLETE AND
UNABRIDGED SERIES
AS PUBLISHED BY
The New York Times

THE PENTAGON PAPERS

BASED ON INVESTIGATIVE REPORTING
BY NEIL SHEEHAN.

WRITTEN BY NEIL SHEEHAN,
HEDRICK SMITH, E. W. KENWORTHY
AND FOX BUTTERFIELD

WITH KEY DOCUMENTS
AND 64 PAGES OF PHOTOGRAPHS

The Pentagon Papers, revealed in the *New York Times*, exposed government wrongdoings during the Vietnam War.

Another government whistle-blower, Daniel Ellsberg, has written extensively about the issue and his belief that Snowden behaved properly. In 1971, Ellsberg was charged under the Espionage Act for the leaking of the Pentagon Papers, a study of US-Vietnam relations over several decades of the twentieth century. Ellsberg had worked on the project, which showed that the United States had been engaged in Vietnam in various forms since the 1940s and that President Johnson had been planning covert operations there long before United States involvement was revealed to the media. Feeling frustrated that the findings of the Pentagon Papers were apparently being ignored by the White House administration, Ellsberg leaked parts to the *New York Times*. He was arrested and faced up to 115 years in prison if found guilty. All criminal charges against him were dropped in 1973, when the Watergate scandal broke and evidence showed that he had been the victim of illegal government wiretapping. Ellsberg has since authored a number of books and has earned numerous awards for his political activism. He remains an outspoken supporter of whistle-blowers, including Manning and Snowden.

When discussing the Snowden case, Ellsberg agreed with his decision to flee the United States. He said that the country had changed a great deal since the 1970s. When Ellsberg was charged, he was allowed to remain free on bond and able to talk openly with the press. He said that similar treatment would not be possible today. He said he believes Snowden would have been arrested and held in isolation with no opportunity for bail. Binney has also suggested that Snowden may have faced torture as a punishment. The chance for a fair, open trial no longer seemed possible. This belief certainly mirrors what happened to Chelsea Manning, who was confined without the opportunity to chat with the media, and who was allowed only one hour of exercise per day, was often not permitted to eat, and was stripped naked, supposedly to prevent suicide attempts.

Ellsberg continued to argue that Snowden has done nothing wrong. In fact, he said that "secrecy corrupts" and that leaks "remain the lifeblood of a free press and our republic." When Snowden began working for the government with security clearance, he took an oath to defend and protect the United States Constitution "against all enemies, foreign and domestic." This oath has been frequently cited by both supporters and critics. In Ellsberg's opinion, by speaking out, Snowden upheld that oath perfectly. He praised Snowden's dedication to the greater good and called him an inspiration to Americans everywhere. Ellsberg also expressed a sense of regret that there were not more whistle-blowers bringing information into the public eye. He said that in the modern age, he would hope to see many more government whistle-blowers.

To Ellsberg, Snowden's actions were those of a patriot. His oath was to defend the Constitution, even if that meant speaking out against the government itself. This raises a debate about patriotism. While nearly everyone would define patriotism as loyalty to one's country, the meaning beyond that is often disputed. Is it blind loyalty to the government and ruling institutions, or does a true patriot show loyalty to the values of a country, even if that places them at odds with the government?

The nature of patriotism has been featured regularly in the news in recent years. In 2016, football player Colin Kaepernick sat, and later knelt, during the playing of the National Anthem at the start of games. He reasoned that he could not "show pride in in a flag for a country that oppresses black people and people of color." His action soon created a nationwide controversy. On the one side were those accusing him of being unpatriotic, some even calling for him to be fired. On the other side were those who argued that patriotism was not about a symbol or a flag, but about raising awareness of injustice. Soon, many other athletes joined him in taking a knee, and numerous military veterans voiced their support. Whether Kaepernick's actions are patriotic or anti-American continues to be discussed.

Journalist Glenn Greenwald often writes strong criticisms of the United States but defines himself as a patriot "to the extent that patriotism means a belief in and a defense of the defining values of your country."

Patriot or Traitor?

Edward Snowden considers himself a patriot above all else. In 2014, he spoke to the media from Russia and said that he misses home and his family, but that he knows he did the right thing. He said that he is being punished for his patriotism and defined that patriotism thus: "Being a patriot means knowing when to protect your country, knowing when to protect your Constitution … Adversaries don't have to be foreign countries. They … can be bad policies. They can be officials who need a little bit more accountability." He also said that it was frustrating to be in a country (Russia) where

Edward Snowden: NSA Contractor and Whistle-Blower

individual human rights and freedoms were not protected, but he said that he could not return home because he would not face a fair trial.

Some politicians have spoken in favor of Snowden's patriotism. While in America, Snowden was a supporter of libertarian candidate Ron Paul in his bid for the presidency. Ron Paul's son Rand is a senator representing Kentucky. In November 2015, Rand Paul praised Edward Snowden for exposing the NSA's surveillance programs. Claiming that the leaks were "a public service," he said, "People are always saying, 'hero or villain?' He is a whistleblower, and he did inform us of something the government's doing that was illegal." This echoed statements Paul had made a year earlier when he argued that Snowden did not deserve to face life in prison for what he had done. He said that the NSA's data collection programs would go down in history as one of the nation's great blunders, along with Japanese-American internment camps and FBI tracking of civil rights leaders and war protestors. What's more, he supported the idea of a class-action lawsuit against the NSA. In February 2014, Paul filed such a lawsuit, on behalf of all Americans who had been affected by the NSA's collection of telephone data. However, the suit was put on hold several months later while several similar cases were also considered.

Despite Paul's praise for Snowden, apparently that patriotism also carried a price tag. The senator said he still believed Snowden should be in prison for breaking the law and revealing government secrets, but that his sentence should be "reasonable and negotiated." Yet, Paul also called for better protections for whistle-blowers.

Rand Paul's opinion seems to suggest that patriotism can and should still be punished when it leads to actions that go against the government. In his view, Snowden was not a traitor seeking to make money by selling secrets. Instead, his actions were a patriotic service to the public, but because he revealed government secrets, even though the secrets were proof of wrongdoing, he should face some type of prison sentence.

Other politicians were less sympathetic toward Snowden. Among those labeling him a traitor are former House Speaker John Boehner and Senator Marco Rubio of Florida. Dick Cheney, who served as vice president under George W. Bush, stated that Snowden was a traitor and that he might have been spying for the Chinese government. Snowden responded that "being called a traitor by Dick Cheney is the highest honor you can give an American." He asked why, if he had been spying for the Chinese, he was not now living a life of luxury in a Beijing palace.

Opposition to Snowden's actions is not limited to those on the Republican side of the political fence. Many Democrats have also voiced their belief that he should be punished as a traitor. Dianne Feinstein, the chair of the Senate Intelligence Committee, said that while there was no evidence of Snowden being a Russian spy, he had committed "an act of treason" and had violated his oath to defend the Constitution. Hillary Clinton criticized him for not following the channels that were in place for whistle-blowers. Had he done so, she suggested, his concerns would have been dealt with. His supporters certainly believe otherwise.

Punishments for Whistle-Blowers

Meanwhile, President Obama, who had once spoken out about the need to protect civil liberties and privacy of Americans, took steps during his time in office to provide harsher penalties for whistle-blowers. *Mother Jones* magazine claimed, "The Obama administration has been cruelly and unusually punishing in its use of the 1917 Espionage Act to stomp on governmental leakers, truth-tellers, and whistleblowers whose disclosures do not support the president's political ambitions." Between 2009 and 2013, his administration cited the Espionage Act in six cases against government whistle-blowers. In late 2012, he announced Presidential Policy Directive 19, supposedly improving protections for whistle-blowers. The NWC opposed the directive because the head of whichever agency the whistle-blower was complaining about would be the one responsible for protecting the person complaining. The organization claimed there was nothing in the directive to encourage people to raise concerns, nor were there any legal protections against the person losing their job.

Despite pardoning Chelsea Manning before the end of his presidency, Obama stated that he could not pardon Snowden since the latter had not gone through any formal court proceedings:

> I think that Mr. Snowden raised some
> legitimate concerns. How he did it
> was something that did not follow the
> procedures and practices of our intelligence
> community. If everybody took the approach

Life for Snowden Today

What is Snowden's life in Moscow like? Although his location is a closely guarded secret, there is little indication that he is living in some stereotypical Cold War apartment. In fact, he told audiences at 2016's San Diego Comic-Con that he lived "a surprisingly free life." In 2015, he denied the common image of Russia being a miserable place, saying, "Russia's great." Both statements seem in stark contrast to early reports that he was living an isolated life of paranoia, afraid to go outside because he would be followed.

Is he living a comfortable life of freedom in Moscow? If so, is that lifestyle a reward for sharing secrets, as some have speculated? Although he claims to be enjoying freedom, it seems naïve that someone with as much experience in surveillance as Snowden would truly believe that his movements are not being monitored.

---

that I make my own decisions about these issues, then it would be very hard to have an organized government or any kind of national security system.

This was questioned by supporters of Snowden, who argued that previous presidents had issued pardons to those who had been indicted but not tried. As an aside, although

President Obama spoke out against Snowden's actions, he did admit that they had led to a national debate that would serve to strengthen the country.

Any hope of a pardon for Snowden evaporated with the end of the Obama presidency. Obama's successor, Donald Trump, repeatedly referred to Snowden as a traitor, even suggesting that he should be executed.

The frequent argument used against Snowden by many politicians is not just that he stole information, but that the information in question put thousands of Americans at risk. Members of the military and those serving around the world in the intelligence field could be endangered. Michael Rogers, director of the NSA in 2015, said that the leaks seriously damaged the nation's surveillance and counterterrorism capabilities. Rogers did not believe that Snowden was a spy for a foreign intelligence agency. He said it was possible that Snowden had received help from Russian agents, knowingly or not. That help might have made it easier for him to obtain some information. Snowden has always claimed that his skills placed him in a position of access to whatever information he wanted, but intelligence officials in Washington have frequently denied that. It is difficult to assess the truth in this situation. It's possible that Snowden might want to make himself appear more heroic and skilled. It's also possible that the government would want to play down his skills to make him seem less important.

Both Rogers and his NSA predecessors have emphasized that Snowden's actions have done immeasurable damage to US intelligence operations. Michael Hayden, who served as NSA director from 1999 to 2006 under Presidents Clinton

Katharine Gun violated the Official Secrets Act after revealing that the NSA had eavesdropped on several United Nations offices in 2003.

and Bush, said that Snowden had done "unquestionable, irreparable, irreversible harm." Rogers and Hayden have further said that the true extent of the damage may not be known for years to come. Hayden explained that to reveal the full extent would be to place the United States at even greater risk.

This raises the question about positive and negative outcomes. While much of the public and media focus has been about how Snowden alerted us to the fact that a government was spying on its own citizens, there is also the issue of what damage it has done. What has been placed at risk, and therefore, what should and shouldn't be leaked?

Snowden has said that it was never his intention to harm US intelligence operations overseas: "I had access to full rosters of anybody working at the NSA. The entire intelligence community and undercover assets around the world ... If I just wanted to damage the US I could have shut down the surveillance system in an afternoon. That was never my intention."

Author Edward Jay Epstein says that his actions opened "a Pandora's box of government secrets":

> Whether Snowden's theft was an idealistic attempt to right a wrong, a narcissistic drive to obtain personal recognition, an attempt to weaken the foundations of the surveillance infrastructure in which he worked or all of the above, by the time he stepped off that Aeroflot jet in Moscow, it had evolved ... into something much simpler and far less admirable. He was disclosing vital national secrets to a foreign power.

Epstein argues that Snowden has shared secrets with Russian intelligence, something the exile has always vehemently denied.

Damage Done?

So what damage has Snowden done? According to Rogers, the leaks have had "a material impact on our ability to generate insights as to what terrorist groups around the world are doing." Given the classified nature of the industry, it is difficult for members of the public to truly assess the extent of the damage, and government officials are unwilling to say too much about it for fear of further damaging international relations and the ongoing work of US intelligence. In 2014, House Intelligence Committee Chair Mike Rogers (not to be confused with NSA Director Michael Rogers) confirmed that Snowden's revelations would probably have "lethal consequences" for American troops. Some have argued that by exposing methods of surveillance, he essentially provided terrorists with a how-to guide for avoiding detection.

The leaks may have also placed British agents at risk. Among the documents released by Edward Snowden were many that related to Government Communications Headquarters (GCHQ), the British security and intelligence organization. Snowden shared information with the *Guardian* about GCHQ's Tempora program. Tempora had been in operation since 2011 and gathered personal internet data by intercepting the signals through fiber-optic cables. Snowden claimed that the Tempora program collected much more metadata on British citizens than the NSA did on Americans. That data was then reportedly shared with the NSA. Whether or not telephone data was also collected as part of Tempora remains unknown; Snowden says yes, but GCHQ says no.

By 2015, the *Sunday Times* was reporting that some British MI6 agents had been recalled from certain countries, for fear that Snowden's leaks had compromised their identities. It was claimed that Russia and China had both obtained files from Snowden and had managed to crack their encryptions. While never confirmed, it is understood that British intelligence has been operating under the assumption that this could have happened. British Foreign Secretary Philip Hammond told reporters that "nobody should be in any doubt that Edward Snowden has caused immense damage." Other British sources claimed it was unreasonable to expect that Russia had not benefited in some way from granting Snowden exile.

Films

On October 24, 2014, Laura Poitras released her film *Citizenfour*, documenting her contact with Edward Snowden and the aftermath of his leaks. At the time of its release, a Hollywood motion picture was already in the planning stages. Director Oliver Stone is well known for his films about twentieth-century American controversies. Some of his previous movies have looked at the assassination of President Kennedy, the Watergate scandal, and the presidency of George W. Bush. He was drawn to the story of the NSA leaks and the man behind them.

Stone first met with Snowden in Russia in January 2014. After two more meetings in May, Snowden agreed to have his story told. In total, the pair would meet on nine separate occasions. The resulting film, simply titled *Snowden*, screened at Comic-Con in the summer of 2016 and premiered in Russia later the same year. To coincide with the release of the film, the American Civil Liberties Union, Amnesty International, and Human Rights Watch launched an ad campaign in the *New York Times*, asking President Obama to issue a pardon. Incidentally, a major intelligence report

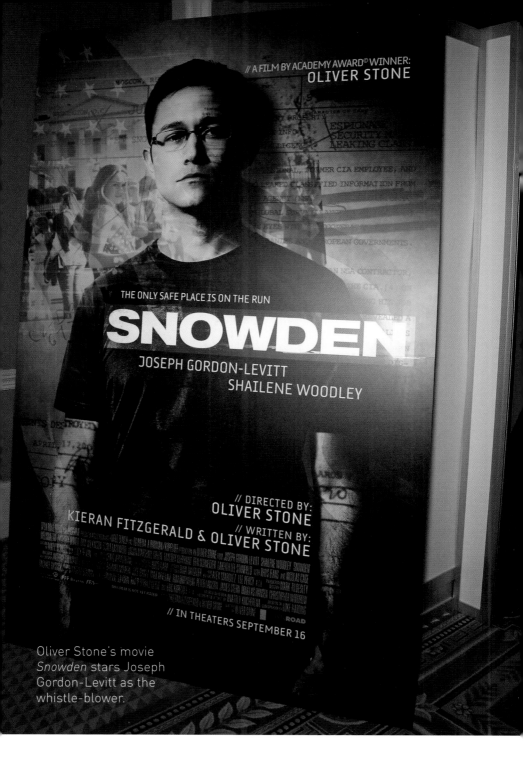

// A FILM BY ACADEMY AWARD® WINNER:
OLIVER STONE

THE ONLY SAFE PLACE IS ON THE RUN

SNOWDEN

JOSEPH GORDON-LEVITT

SHAILENE WOODLEY

// DIRECTED BY:
OLIVER STONE
KIERAN FITZGERALD & OLIVER STONE
// WRITTEN BY:

// IN THEATERS SEPTEMBER 16

Oliver Stone's movie
Snowden stars Joseph
Gordon-Levitt as the
whistle-blower.

detailing some of the damages alleged to have resulted from Snowden's actions was released on the same day.

In *Snowden*, Stone is unwavering in his portrayal of the titular character as a patriot. Speaking in defense of the whistle-blower's actions, Stone said: "No one in America has signed a contract that allows the government to probe into your life. It's so antithetical to what the American Revolution was about, where what was important was individual sovereignty and limited [government]." Although Stone claimed that his film would do more to publicize Snowden's case than anything else had, *Snowden* was a commercial failure. It also received mixed critical reviews.

Tech Support

Within the tech world, a great deal of support was voiced for Edward Snowden. In a 2016 opinion piece for CNN, Jimmy Wales, cofounder of the Wikipedia website, called him "a saint, not a sinner." He went on to explain that Wikipedia was intended to be a politically neutral site, but one where information could be freely and openly exchanged. He said that Snowden's actions followed those same principles and gave people the ability to protect themselves and to reclaim the internet, free from being spied on. Wales reasoned, "Without him, ordinary people around the world would still know little of the growing dragnet stifling the Internet's enormous potential for good." As a result of the leaks, Wales believes that the internet has become a safer place for people. Sites have improved their encryption methods to better protect people's personal data.

Wales did warn that there had also been negative results to Snowden's actions, the main one being that people were now more wary of what they should do online. While in some respects this has been a good thing, it has also resulted in "unprecedented levels of self-censorship." In the long run, according to Wales, history will recognize Snowden as a hero.

Fellow tech giant Steve Wozniak has echoed this sentiment. The cofounder of Apple has praised Snowden for being "a total hero." He went on to say that the whistle-blower "gave up his own life … to help the rest of us." He compared his actions to those of Daniel Ellsberg, claiming that they were driven by a true belief in the Constitution, democracy, and freedom.

One strong voice of disagreement has been Bill Gates, the billionaire founder of Microsoft. While fellow members of the computer industry were hailing Snowden as a hero, Gates labeled him a criminal:

> I think he broke the law, so I certainly wouldn't characterize him as a hero. If he wanted to raise the issues and stay in the country and engage in civil disobedience or something of that kind, or if he had been careful in terms of what he had released, then it would fit more of the model of "OK, I'm really trying to improve things." You won't find much admiration from me.

Gates did see a need for debate about what technology was capable of, and what purposes it should be used for. He has called for "more explicit rules" about what is and isn't available online.

Negative Effects and Public Opinion

Interestingly, despite strong support from many sectors of the technology industry, there may be negative business effects from overseas. Some foreign companies have expressed a reluctance to use American firms such as Microsoft or Google for fear that the security of their data might be compromised. The part played by tech and communication firms in the gathering of the data has often been cause for debate. Many companies have said publicly that they oppose such collection, while some leaks from Snowden suggested that companies such as AT&T or Verizon may have been perfectly willing to participate.

What about the American public? How do they view Edward Snowden? Is he a hero for making them aware that their government was collecting information about them, or is he a villain, placing post-9/11 America in further danger? According to a 2015 poll commissioned by the ACLU, 64 percent of Americans had a negative view of him. Only 36 percent looked at him positively. This was in stark contrast to some other nations. For example, 84 percent of Germans and Italians had a positive opinion of Snowden, as well as 80 percent of Dutch, French, and Spanish citizens. The results among those polled in the United States varied significantly by age, with more millennials supporting him.

This support among the younger demographic was also demonstrated in a survey released in January 2014. Adults under the age of thirty were more likely to see Snowden as having served the public good. As to whether he should be prosecuted, young adults were divided fairly evenly.

Support may be waning over time, however. A poll in late 2016 found that just 15 percent of those surveyed would call him a hero. Thirty percent considered him a traitor, while 48 percent answered that it was complicated, placing him somewhere between the two. With regards to prosecution, only 25 percent favored a pardon, with 43 percent wanting to see him face treason charges.

Is it possible that Snowden can be both hero and villain? William Binney seems to have suggested so. Snowden stole, in all likelihood, more than one million classified documents. As far as we know, only a portion was shared with Greenwald, Poitras, and MacAskill, and so only a small segment became public. That assumes that the material has not fallen into enemy hands. It also fails to take into account that some of the information was internationally damaging. When he first reached out to the media, his actions seem to have been triggered by a legitimate desire to serve the public good. One might argue that these pieces of information about metadata collection and surveillance of US citizens were "legitimately leakable." At a certain point, the leaks continued to pour forth as if through a busted dam. As Binney notes, some of these were no longer for the public good but were damaging. For example, was there a legitimate public service aspect in the revelations about bugging Angela Merkel's phone or hacking Chinese government databases? Did these leaks move Snowden from the realm of public hero to something more treacherous?

Deep Throat and Watergate

In June 1972, five men were arrested for breaking into the offices of the Democratic National Committee in the Watergate building in Washington, DC. A few days later, a secret informant began talking to two journalists at the *Washington Post*, Bob Woodward and Carl Bernstein. The informant, nicknamed Deep Throat by the newspaper's editor, provided information that linked the break-in to a number of high-ranking people within the White House. This would eventually lead to the beginnings of an impeachment process against President Richard Nixon and his resignation in 1974.

For many years, the identity of Deep Throat remained a mystery. A movie was made about the events leading up to the president's resignation, and many books and articles speculated who Deep Throat might be. Some even thought it could be President Nixon himself.

The secret was revealed in 2005. Deep Throat was Mark Felt, the former associate director of the FBI. Unlike Edward Snowden, he had gone to great lengths to protect his identity, repeatedly denying his role. Both before and after the revelation, public opinion was divided. To some, Felt was a patriotic hero, committed to uncovering the truth. To others, he was a traitor, angry that he had not been chosen to serve as FBI director and determined to bring down the agency so that he could step in and rebuild its reputation. Felt died in 2008.

Watergate has left a lasting legacy on both American politics and journalism. It damaged the American public's trust in the White House. Previously, there had been little reason to question the honesty of the country's leaders. The scandal also showed that no one is immune from their wrongdoings—whether real or imagined, as Nixon was never definitively linked to the break-in—not even the president.

Modern technology makes electronic surveillance easier than ever.

Summing Up

Historically speaking, it has been a relatively short time since an unknown Booz Allen Hamilton employee in Hawaii called in sick to work, boarded a plane to Hong Kong, and prepared to expose the biggest classified-document leak in US history. In that short time, a great deal has changed with regards to technology, awareness of personal privacy, and national security.

Edward Snowden has become a household name throughout much of the West. What has been his lasting legacy, or is it still too soon to tell?

The Good, the Bad, and the Ugly

Edward Jay Epstein, a political science professor and investigative journalist, has categorized the consequences of Snowden's actions into three main subsets: the good, the bad, and the ugly. The good is that the leaks have led to important public conversations about personal privacy and about the government overstepping boundaries. He asks whether the problem is the surveillance itself or what is done with the metadata that is collected. Epstein also praises the leaks for having led to modifications of the Patriot Act. He goes on to list the bad consequences, primarily the profound damage to the US intelligence community, the full extent of which may never be known. Lastly, there are what Epstein refers to as the ugly consequences—a huge erosion of people's trust in the government and in politicians.

Other Effects: Positive and Negative

It is almost indisputable that the conversation about personal privacy was much needed and long overdue. Jimmy Wales praised Snowden for pushing the debate, which he says has made the internet a safer place. He says that young people are now much more careful about what they share online, aware that it can be collected and stored indefinitely. Wales says:

> A brave young American whistleblower has given us the most important tool in our fight to reclaim the Internet: knowledge. Snowden acted out of a love of the Internet and its promise as an open space for collaboration, sharing and experimentation. I'd like to think that if I had been in his place, I would have done the same thing.

For his act of conscience, he deserves our overwhelming appreciation.

In addition to people gaining more awareness of personal privacy issues with regards to technology, there have also been direct changes in NSA data collection practices. In December 2013, Richard Leon, a senior federal judge in the District of Columbia, ruled that the bulk collection of phone records probably violated the Fourth Amendment to the Constitution. Describing the practice as "almost Orwellian" in scope, he ruled:

> The Government does not cite a single instance in which analysis of the NSA's bulk metadata collection actually stopped an imminent attack ... Because of the utter lack of evidence that a terrorist act has ever been prevented because searching the NSA database was faster than other investigative tactics—I have serious doubts about the efficacy of the metadata collection program.

Leon concluded his opinion by stating that "the author of our Constitution, James Madison, would be aghast."

In May 2015, a Congressional vote to reform the Patriot Act put an official end to the NSA's collection of metadata. In passing the USA Freedom Act, Congress extended some parts of the Patriot Act that were due to expire. They also recognized the need to rein in some of the government's surveillance methods and to be more transparent to the public. This was a direct result of Edward Snowden's actions.

Snowden's revelations have raised public awareness about electronic surveillance by the NSA.

Proponents of the bipartisan bill said it was important to restore order to programs that had gone too far. Civil liberties advocates said it still did not go far enough. Experts in the field concur, saying that large numbers of the surveillance programs remain in operation. They argue that once the furor of Snowden's revelations died down, very little real change took place.

Snowden's actions did do severe damage to US intelligence agencies, however. They also created cracks in some foreign relations. The director of the National Counterterrorism Center, Nicholas Rasmussen, testified to Congress in early 2015 that Snowden has limited capabilities to do any real damage to national intelligence. Quite simply, he had revealed their playbook. However, other consequences of Snowden's actions may never be known, as the full depth of the data he released has not been determined. Due to the highly classified nature of the intelligence business, the public would probably never know, for example, if an agent in the field were exposed and killed.

Then there is Epstein's "ugly consequence"—a growing mistrust of the government. Can we attribute this only to Edward Snowden? Was Snowden the originator of such dissatisfaction, or were his actions a reflection of society's feelings? Since the September 11 attacks, the United States has struggled with paranoia and xenophobia. Conspiracy theories have flooded the internet. Among them are beliefs that the government knew about the planned attacks in advance but did nothing; the towers were demolished in a manner to suggest a terrorist attack; the damage to the Pentagon was caused by an intentional US missile; and more. Much of this stemmed from a sense of disbelief that such a thing could happen in the United States. How could no one have foreseen such a situation? Disbelief and grief led to fear and anger. Over the years, these have built into dissatisfaction and the bittersweet joke that America is always being watched. Such sentiments certainly did not originate with Snowden. His actions did bring them to the forefront of public discussion though.

The Changing Tactics of Journalism

What of the journalists who broke the story? In October 2013, just a few months after breaking the Snowden story, Glenn Greenwald left the *Guardian* to establish the *Intercept*, an online news publication dedicated to independent journalism. Laura Poitras is his coeditor. Poitras also went on to make another documentary after the award-winning *Citizenfour*. The 2016 documentary *Risk* was about WikiLeaks founder Julian Assange. In 2014, Greenwald, Poitras, and Ewen MacAskill all received the Polk Award for National Security Reporting in honor of their work on the Snowden story. Like his two colleagues, the latter still works in political journalism. MacAskill has paid tribute to Snowden for the changes he brought about in public debate and in communications: "If Snowden has a lasting legacy beyond the surveillance vs. privacy debate, it is that there is much more awareness now among the public, but especially among journalists, about security of communications. More and more journalists are shifting to encrypted communication."

Edward Snowden appears via video-link at San Diego's Comic-Con in July 2016 for a screening of Oliver Stone's *Snowden*.

The change to encrypted communications has altered the way in which journalism is conducted. As more publications and sources have switched to online formats, the need for greater security measures has become more evident. Whether the Snowden story would have or could have broken in the way it did had he not insisted on sophisticated encryption methods remains a mystery.

The case of Edward Snowden has also changed what is revealed by journalists and when. For many decades, it was fairly common practice for government agencies to request that a newspaper hold off on a story or not publish it at all, if it was deemed risky to national security. This was reinforced after September 11 with an unspoken sense of patriotic protectionism. That has changed. Although just a small portion of the documents Snowden obtained was released to the public through the media, for months it seemed like an unending avalanche of new revelations. One story after another came, and soon even the slightest sliver of information was a story in its own right. The government has responded accordingly. Realizing the magnitude of the data, intelligence agencies took an alternative approach, engaging in what some have called "a charm offensive." The NSA released some of their own reports and seemed aware of the need to reform, at least in the public eye.

Snowden Now

What of the whistle-blower himself? At the time of this writing, Edward Snowden still lives in Russia. He has expressed a desire to return to the United States but will only do so if he does not face espionage charges. For now, he seems content to remain in Moscow. He participates regularly in technology conferences via video link, and he serves as president of the Freedom of the Press Foundation, a small nonprofit organization based in San Francisco. The goal of the organization is to help protect journalists and

Snowden supporters in France made signs of his face at a rally in 2013.

their sources. Modern technological surveillance would make it all too easy to track a journalist and hence, their sources. Snowden and the foundation staff are putting their tech skills to use. Snowden is working to create a security modification that can detect cell phone malware that might give out location information. He is also working on a newsroom encryption program and a protected video chat software. No doubt inspired by Greenwald's lack of encryption knowledge, the intent is to produce a series of programs that members of the press can easily use without the need for advanced computer knowledge.

When Greenwald first met Snowden, he remarked how the young man seemed to see himself in terms of a video game hero. In video games, there is a clear demarcation between good and bad, between the hero and the villain. Perhaps this is how Snowden saw himself, as the hero protecting the world from the evil spy overlords. In the real world, things are not always so clearly separated. The actions of both the hero and the villain may become blurred. There may be influences and consequences that are unknown. Issues such as national security, personal freedom, and the possible tradeoff between the two complicate matters, leaving uncertainty as to who the real heroes or villains may be.

While there are some definitive changes that have come about as a result of Snowden's actions, there are some that will remain unknown. This means judgments can only be made based on the information that is given. Having read about his actions, and some of the responses to them, is Edward Snowden a hero, a villain, or is the truth still somewhere in between?

asylum Protection given by a country to someone who has been forced to flee their home country because of political persecution.

contact chaining The use of computer algorithms to identify telephone numbers or email addresses that a particular number or email address has been in contact with.

cyberattacks A deliberate attempt by hackers to break into and damage a computer system.

eavesdrop To secretly listen to the private conversations of other people.

encryption The conversion of data into a code so that it can only be read by others with access to the same code.

espionage The use of spies to obtain secret data.

extradition One country's decision to return a person to another country where they have been charged with a crime, usually following a formal request.

FISA The Foreign Intelligence Surveillance Act. Federal legislation enacted in 1978 to establish a series of rules and procedures for wiretapping and other surveillance methods.

intelligence Information regarding the political and military knowledge and actions of another country or possible enemy.

Glossary

metadata Data that provides information about other data. In this context, it is usually referring to records of telephone calls, email communications, and other electronic transactions.

national security The protection of a country's people, economy, and government.

oversight Carefully watching and monitoring to make sure something is done properly and in accordance with guidelines.

Patriot Act An act of Congress signed into law in October 2001 in response to the September 11 terrorist attacks. It laid out a series of procedures and rules to help prevent terrorist attacks and strengthen the security of the United States.

refugee Someone who has been forced to flee their home country, usually due to war or fear of political, religious, racial, or economic persecution, and who is unable to return.

Stellar Wind An NSA program to conduct mass data collection of communications by American citizens without the correct court warrants.

surveillance Close observation and monitoring of a person's actions and communications.

1983

Edward Joseph Snowden is born in North Carolina.

2001

Terrorist attacks on New York and Washington, DC. Project Stellar Wind begins mass data collection. President George W. Bush signs the Patriot Act into law.

2003

The United States invades Iraq.

2004

Snowden enlists in the military. He is discharged in September before completing his training.

2006

Snowden gains employment as an analyst with the CIA Global Communications Division.

2007

Snowden spends six months in Geneva.

Chronology

2009

Snowden resigns from the CIA and takes a position with Dell at their NSA facility in Tokyo, Japan.

2011

Snowden returns to the United States and works at the Dell facility in Maryland.

2012

Snowden begins illegally downloading classified documents and sends an encrypted email in the first of many attempts to contact Glenn Greenwald.

2013

Snowden boards a flight to Hong Kong to meet with Glenn Greenwald and Laura Poitras. The *Guardian* runs the first article related to Snowden's leaks and the NSA spying on American citizens.

2013

The US Justice Department files espionage and theft against Snowden. He is then granted asylum in Russia.

Books

Edgar, Timothy H. *Beyond Snowden: Privacy, Mass Surveillance, and the Struggle to Reform the NSA.* Washington, DC: Brookings Institution Press, 2017.

Epstein, Edward Jay. *How America Lost Its Secrets: Edward Snowden, the Man and the Theft.* New York: Alfred A. Knopf, 2017.

Ewing, Alphonse B, ed. *The USA Patriot Act Reader.* London, UK: Nova Science Publishing, 2005.

Goldfarb, Ronald, ed. *After Snowden: Privacy, Secrecy, and Security in the Information Age.* New York: Thomas Dunne Books, 2015.

Harding, Luke. *The Snowden Files: The Inside Story of the World's Most Wanted Man.* New York: Vintage Books, 2014.

Rall, Ted. *Snowden.* New York: Seven Stories Press, 2015.

Websites

American Civil Liberties Union
https://www.aclu.org/
The ACLU's goal is to protect individual liberties as guaranteed by the Constitution. The site contains information about personal privacy and related issues.

Free Snowden

https://edwardsnowden.com/

This site raises awareness and support for Edward Snowden and publicizes issues raised by his whistle-blowing.

National Security Agency

https://www.nsa.gov/

This official site includes the history and ongoing work of the NSA.

National Whistleblower Center

https://www.whistleblowers.org

The official home of the National Whistleblower Center offers legal and historical information about the importance of whistle-blowing in the United States.

The *Intercept*

https://theintercept.com

This is the news site founded by Glenn Greenwald, Laura Poitras, and Jeremy Scahill.

The NSA Files

https://www.theguardian.com/us-news/the-nsa-files

This is a collection of the various NSA-related stories that appeared in the *Guardian*.

Bamford, Jason. "Edward Snowden: The Untold Story." *Wired*, August 2014. https://www.wired.com/2014/08/edward-snowden.

Bhaskar, Shiva. "The Mixed Legacy of Edward Snowden." *Medium*, October 30, 2015. https://medium.com/@shivagbhaskar/the-mixed-legacy-of-edward-snowden-6b10080c27db.

Boehme, Gerry. *Edward Snowden: Heroic Whistleblower or Traitorous Spy?* New York: Cavendish Square Publishing, 2017.

Boot, Eric R. "Classified Public Whistleblowing: How to Justify a Pro Tanto Wrong." *Social Theory and Practice*, 43:3 (2017): 541-567.

Cassidy, John. "Snowden's Legacy: A Public Debate About Online Privacy." *New Yorker*, August 20, 2013. https://www.newyorker.com/news/john-cassidy/snowdens-legacy-a-public-debate-about-online-privacy.

Coddington, Andrew. *Mass Government Surveillance: Spying on Citizens.* New York: Cavendish Square Publishing, 2017.

Crowdus, Gary. "Edward Snowden is Not Your Average Hero." *Cineaste*, Winter 2016, Vol. 42 Issue 1: 22-30.

Ellsberg, Daniel. "NSA leaker Snowden made the right call." *Washington Post*, July 7, 2013. https://www.washingtonpost.com/opinions/ daniel-ellsberg-nsa-leaker-snowden-made-the-right-call/2013/07/07/0b46d96c-e5b7-11e2-aef3-339619eab080_story.html?utm_term=. f6407ab97b7b.

Epstein, Edward J. "The Edward Snowden Files." *Newsweek*, January 20, 2017.

Fidler, David P., ed. *The Snowden Reader*. Bloomington: Indiana University Press, 2015.

Friedersdorf, Conor. "Daniel Ellsberg: Snowden Kept His Oath Better Than Anyone in the NSA." *Atlantic*, July 25, 2014. https://www.theatlantic. com/politics/archive/2014/07/daniel-ellsberg-snowden-honored-his-oath-better-than-anyone-in-the-nsa/375031.

Gardner, Lloyd C. *The War on Leakers: National Security and American Democracy, from Eugene V. Debs to Edward Snowden*. New York: The New Press, 2016.

Gray, David. *The Fourth Amendment in an Age of Surveillance.* New York: Cambridge University Press, 2017.

Greenwald, Glenn. *No Place to Hide: Edward Snowden, the NSA and the U.S. Surveillance State.* New York: Metropolitan Books, 2014.

Harmon, Daniel E. *21st Century Surveillance Technologies.* New York: Cavendish Square Publishing, 2017.

Kendzior, Sarah. "Snowden and the Paranoid State." Al Jazeera, August 5, 2013. http://www.aljazeera.com/indepth/opinion/2013/08/2013858490192123.html.

MacAskill, Ewen. "The Perfect Source: Edward Snowden, a Role Model for Whistleblowers and Journalists Everywhere." Ethics in the News. Ethical Journalism Network. http://ethicaljournalismnetwork.org/resources/publications/ethics-in-the-news/edward-snowden.

Nolan, Cynthia. "The Edward Snowden Case and the Morality of Secrecy." *Catholic Social Science Review*, 22 (2017): 291-310.

Paterniti, Michael. "The Man Who Knew Too Much." *GQ*, May 11, 2014. https://www.gq.com/story/glenn-greenwald-edward-snowden-no-place-to-hide.

Poitras, Laura. *Citizenfour.* Documentary. 2014.
Praxis Films, Participant Media, and HBO
Documentary Films.

Reitman, Janet. "Snowden and Greenwald: The Men
Who Leaked the Secrets." *Rolling Stone*, December
4, 2013. https://www.rollingstone.com/politics/news/
snowden-and-greenwald-the-men-who-leaked-the-
secrets-20131204.

Small, Cathleen. *Surveillance and Your Right to Privacy.*
New York: Cavendish Square Publishing, 2018.

Stein, Jeff. "No Country for Edward Snowden."
Newsweek, October 14, 2016.

Van Buren, Peter. "Obama's War on Whistleblowers."
Mother Jones, June 12, 2012. http://www.motherjones.
com/politics/2012/06/obamas-whistleblowers-
stuxnet-leaks-drones/.

Weinger, Mackenzie. "Snowden's Impact Fades After
Three Years." Cipher Brief, June 5, 2016. https://www.
thecipherbrief.com/snowdens-impact-fades-after-
three-years-2.

Page numbers in **boldface** are illustrations.

Afghanistan, 16–17, 32, 50
air travel, 17
Alexander, Keith, 30–31
American Civil Liberties Union (ACLU), 24–25, 80, 84
Assange, Julian, 50–51, 95
asylum, 10, 49–51, 54

Bamford, James, 30
Binney, William, 25–27, 47, 62, 64–65, 67, 85
Booz Allen Hamilton, 9, 38–39, 89
Bush, George W., 16, 18, 27–28, **29**, 73, 77, 80

Central Intelligence Agency (CIA), 9, **10**, 11, 19, 21, 30, 37–38, 41, 58
Church Committee, 19, 21
Citizenfour (film), 44, 80, 95
Citizenfour (pseudonym), 42–43
Clapper, James, 31
contact chaining, 22–24, 32, 64
cyberattacks, 30

decryption, 18, 25
Dell, 9, 38
Department of Defense, 11, 26, 64–65
Department of Homeland Security, 18, 32
Department of Justice, 22, 32, 49, 64
Drake, Thomas, 62, 64–65

eavesdrop, 15, 26–28, 31, 39
Ellsberg, Daniel, 67–68, 83
encryption, 11, 41–44, 79, 82, 95–97, 99
Epstein, Edward Jay, 78, 89–90, 94
espionage, 50, 65, 97
Espionage Act of 1917, 10, 49, 62, 67, 74
extradition, 49–51

Federal Bureau of Investigation (FBI), 6, 19, 25, 31, 37, 64, 72, 86–87
FISA Amendments Act (FAA), 28, **29**, 30, 32
Foreign Intelligence Surveillance Act (FISA), 21–22, 28, 32
Fourth Amendment, 18–19, 23, 25, 91
Freedom of the Press Foundation, 97, 99

Gates, Bill, 83–84
GCHQ, 45, 79
Gellman, Barton, 47–48
Greenwald, Glenn, 5, 39, **40**, 41–45, 47–49, 53, 57–58, 69, 84, 95, 99
Guantanamo, 18
Guardian, the, 5, 10, 33, 41, 43, 47–48, 53, 57, 79, 95

Hayden, Michael, 30, 76–77
Hong Kong, 9, 39, 43–44, 49–51, 53, 55, 57, 89

Index

intelligence, 5, 11, 21, 28, 35,
37, 41, 43, 45, 50, 54–55,
73–76, 78–80, 90, 94, 97
Intercept, the, 95
Iraq, 16–17, 36, 41, 50

Kaepernick, Colin, 69

MacAskill, Ewen, 43–44, 48,
53, 58, 85, 95
Manning, Chelsea, 47, 50, 62,
63, 67–68, 74
Merkel, Angela, 55, 85
metadata, 11, 19, 22, 26–27, 33,
47, 79, 85, 90–91
Moscow, Russia, 10, 51, **52**,
53–55, 75, 78, 97

national security, 6, 11, 14, 18,
21–24, 27–28, 61–62, 65, 75,
89, 95, 97, 99
National Security Agency
(NSA), 5, 9–11, 18–19, 21–22,
24–28, 30–33, 38, 41, 45,
47–48, 55, 62, 64–65, 72, 76,
78–80, 91, 97
New York Times, 5–6, 24, 27, 48,
67, 80

Obama, Barack, 30, 33, 44–45,
50, 74–76, 80
oversight, 21–22, 27, 30

Patriot Act, 24–25, 31–32,
90–91
patriotism, 36, 68–69, 72–73,
82, 86, 97
Paul, Rand, **70–71**, 72–73
Paul, Ron, 24, 36, 72
Pentagon Papers, **66**, 67

Poitras, Laura, 39, 41–45, **42**,
47–49, 53, 58–59, 80, 85, 95
privacy, 6, 11, 14–15, 17, 23–25,
27–28, 30, 45, 65, 74, 89–91,
95
Project Minaret, 19

refugee, 49
Rogers, Michael, 76–78

September 11 attacks, 6, 10,
12, 13–15, 17–18, 24, 26–27,
64–65, 84, 94, 97
Stellar Wind, 24, 26, 32, 45
Stone, Oliver, 80, 82
Supreme Court, 23
surveillance, 10, 17–19, 21–25,
27–28, 30, 41, 45, 48, 65, 72,
75–76, 78–79, 85, 90–91,
94–95, 99

Tempora, 79
Tokyo, Japan, 9, 38
Trailblazer, 62, 64–65

United Nations, 49

Vietnam War, 19, 67

Wales, Jimmy, 82–83, 90–91
war on terror, 16–17, **16**, 22, 32,
41, 55
warrants, 19, 22–23, 25–28,
30–31, 41
Watergate, 67, 80, 86–87
whistle-blower, definition of,
59, 61
Wiebe, J. Kirk, 62, 64
WikiLeaks, 50, 95
Wozniak, Steve, 83

Fiona Young-Brown is the author of multiple books, including *Nuclear Fusion and Fission*; *The Universe to Scale: Similarities and Differences in Objects in our Solar System*; *Sudan*; and *Eleanor Roosevelt: First Lady*. Originally from the United Kingdom, she lives with her husband and dogs in Kentucky.